© 2005 by Lynn Lusby Pratt
refuge™ is a trademark of Standard Publishing.
EMPOWERED® Youth Products is a trademark of Standard Publishing.
All rights reserved. Printed in China.

Standard Publishing, Cincinnati, Ohio.
A division of Standex International Corporation.

Cover and interior photography: David Strasser
Cover and interior design: Robert Glover
Project editor: Dale Reeves

Scripture quotations marked NLT are taken from the Holy Bible, *New Living Translation*, copyright © 1996. Used by permission of Tyndale House Publishers, Inc., Wheaton, Illinois 60189. All rights reserved.
Scripture quotations marked NIV are taken from the HOLY BIBLE, NEW INTERNATIONAL VERSION®. NIV®. Copyright © 1973, 1978, 1984 by International Bible Society. Used by permission of Zondervan. All rights reserved.
Scripture quotations marked THE MESSAGE are taken from *The Message*, copyright © by Eugene H. Peterson, 1993, 1994, 1995. Used by permission of NavPress Publishing Group.

12 11 10 09 08 07 06 05

7 6 5 4 3 2 1

ISBN 0-7847-1777-X

Beyond is designed both for reflecting on present life and for moving beyond—toward the future. Perhaps you will decide to bury a bad habit, resurrect a forgotten talent, lay to rest a destructive relationship or bring to life something new. Rest assured, God has amazing plans—for now and forever—to give you a life *beyond* anything you could ask or imagine.

> "My life is my message."
> —Mahatma Ghandi

EPITAPH

Beneath this stone
a lump of clay
Lies Uncle Peter Daniels.
Who too early
in the month of May
Took off his winter
flannels.

—unknown

> "No eye has seen, no ear has heard, and no mind has imagined
> what God has prepared for those who love him."
>
> —1 Corinthians 2:9, NLT

"I intend to live forever. So far, so good."
—Steven Wright

"The LORD God formed the man from the dust of the ground and breathed into his nostrils the breath of life, and the man became a living being."
—Genesis 2:7, NIV

"[THE ANGELS HAVE] HAD A LOT
OF PRACTICE AT WORSHIPING. . . .
THEY'VE SEEN IT ALL. YET WHEN WE
ARRIVE IN HEAVEN, IT WILL BE THEIR
PRIVILEGE TO WORSHIP WITH US."
—JONI EARECKSON TADA

HERE LIES THE BODY...

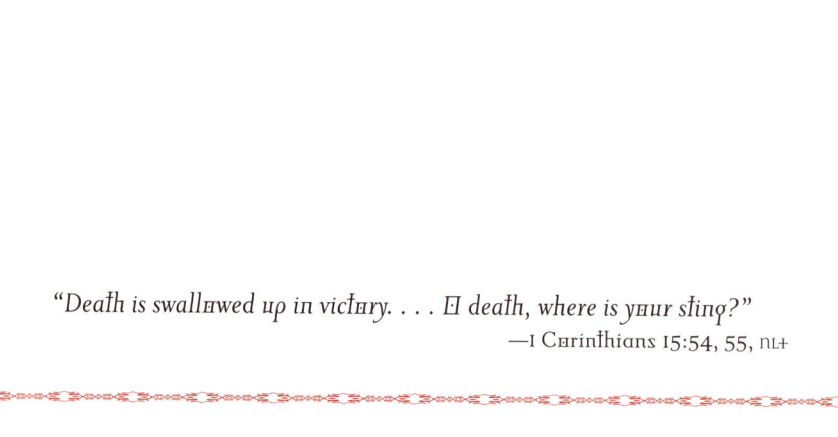

> "Death is swallowed up in victory. . . . O death, where is your sting?"
> —1 Corinthians 15:54, 55, NLT

"GOD, YOU WARNED ME IT WOULD BE THIS WAY.
THIS IS MY LIFE WHEN I CHOOSE TO TURN AWAY.
BUT THIS ISN'T WHAT YOU MEANT FOR MY LIFE."
—ANDREA SUMMER

> ### ⚘ EPITAPH ⚘
> Against his will
> Here lies GEORGE HILL
> Who from a cliff
> Fell down quite stiff;
> When it happened
> is not known,
> Therefore not mention'd
> on this stone.
> —Churchyard in Isle of Thanet

> "Live every day like it's your last,
> 'cause one day you're gonna be right."
> —Ray Charles

"I am the Alpha and the Omega,
the First and the Last,
the Beginning and the End."
—Jesus, Revelation 22:13, NIV

"The only way to have a life is to commit to it like crazy."
—Angelina Jolie

"My purpose is to give life in all its fullness."
—Jesus, John 10:10, NLT

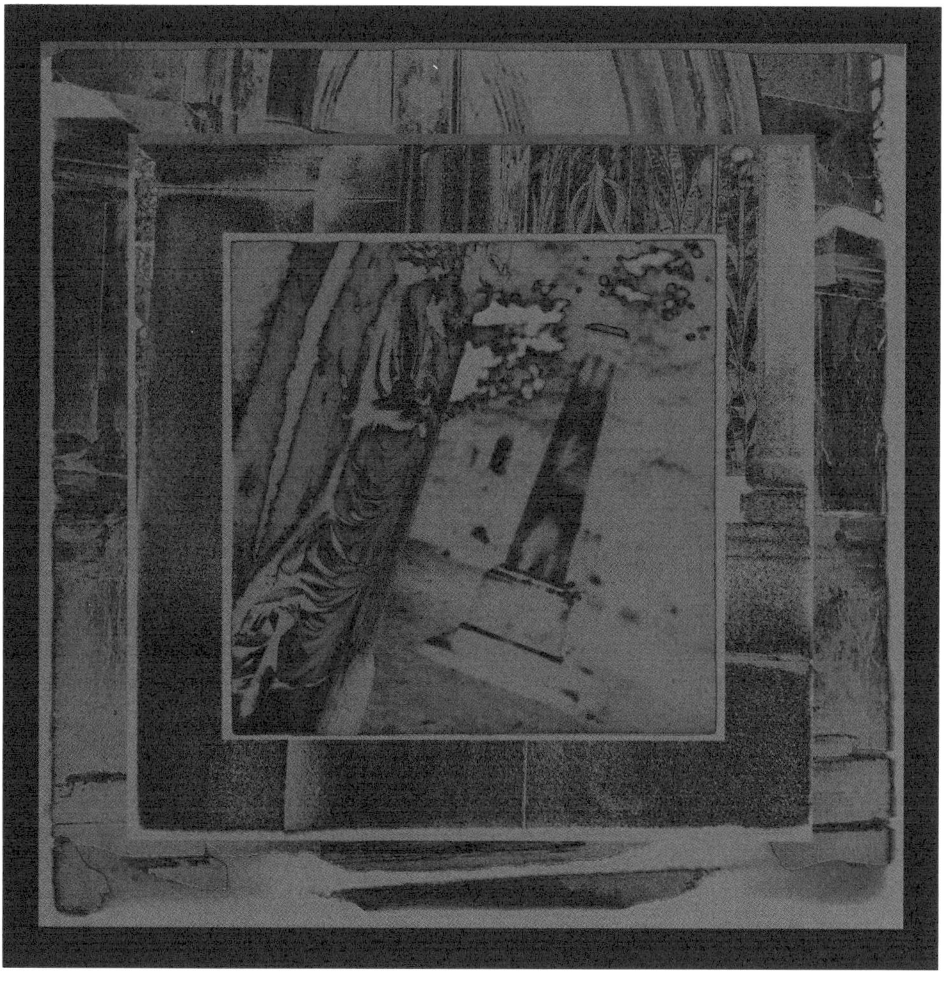

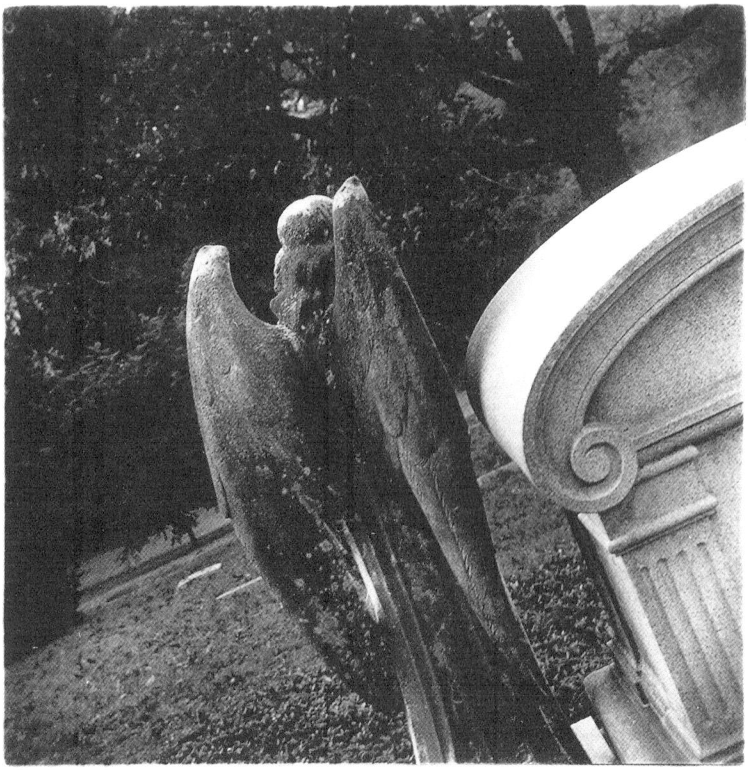

"The Lord himself will come down from heaven with a commanding shout, with the call of the archangel, and with the trumpet call of God. First, all the Christians who have died will rise from their graves. Then, together with them, we who are still alive and remain on the earth will be caught up in the clouds to meet the Lord in the air and remain with him forever."

—1 Thessalonians 4:16, 17, NLT

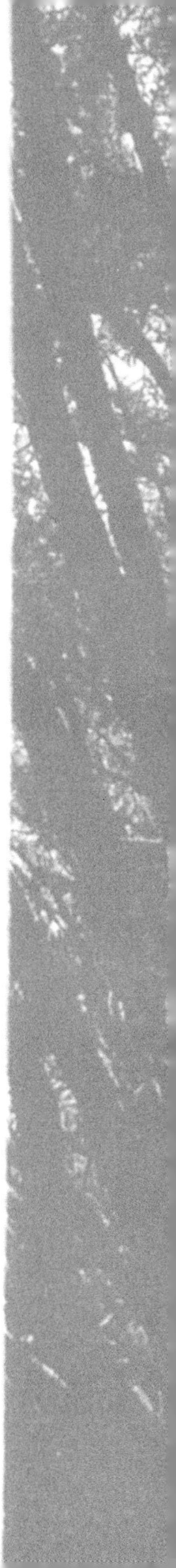

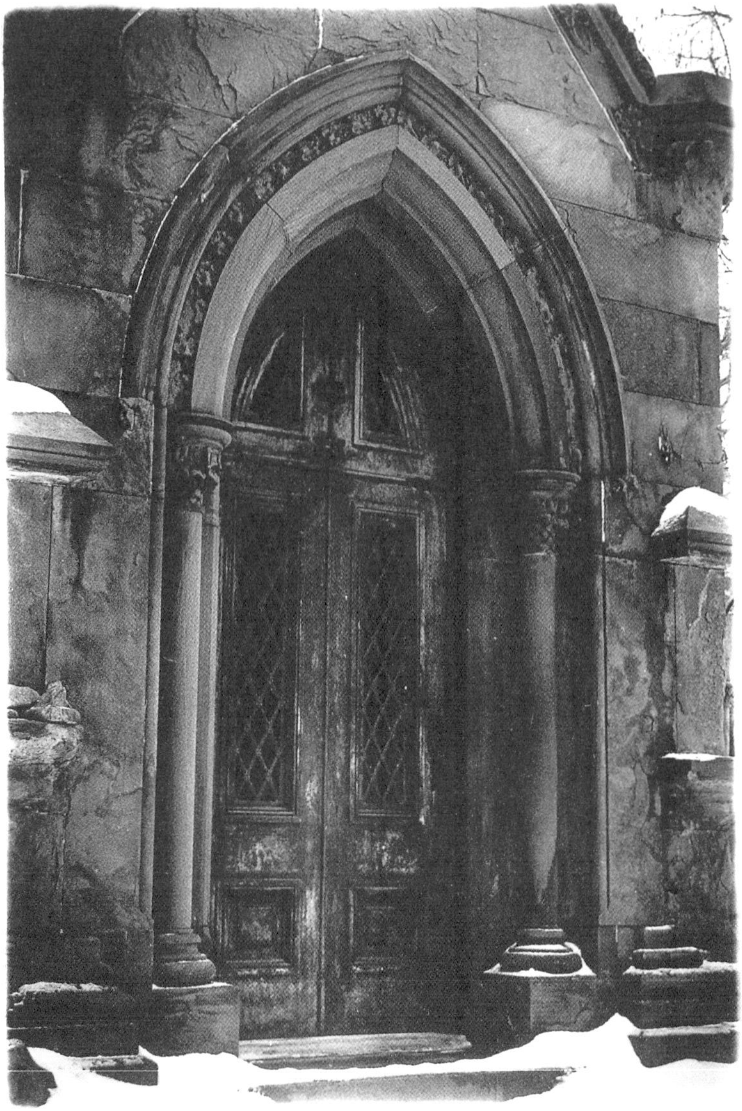

> "I'M SO NOT READY TO DIE. IT PETRIFIES ME. I GO ALONE. I GO TO A PLACE I DON'T KNOW. IT MIGHT BE PAINFUL. IT MIGHT BE THE END. MY THOUGHT IS THAT IT IS THE END."
>
> —William Shatner (best known as Captain Kirk on *Star Trek*)

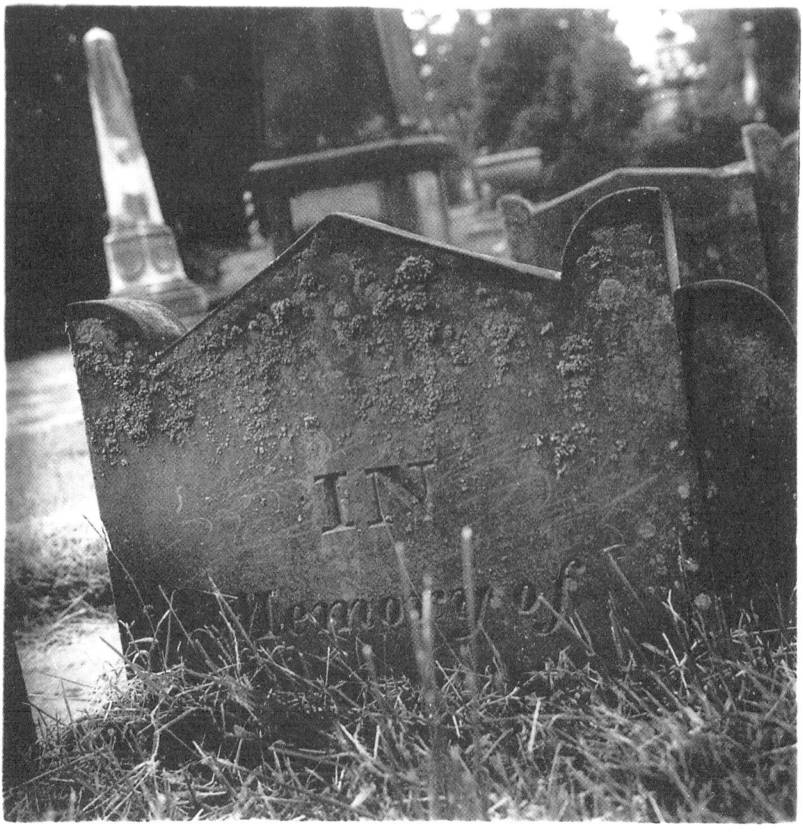
IN

"Life is what happens to you while you're busy making other plans."
—John Lennon

Rise again

"I didn't die. I lived! And now I'm telling the world what God did. God tested me, he pushed me hard, but he didn't hand me over to Death."

—Psalm 118:17, THE MESSAGE

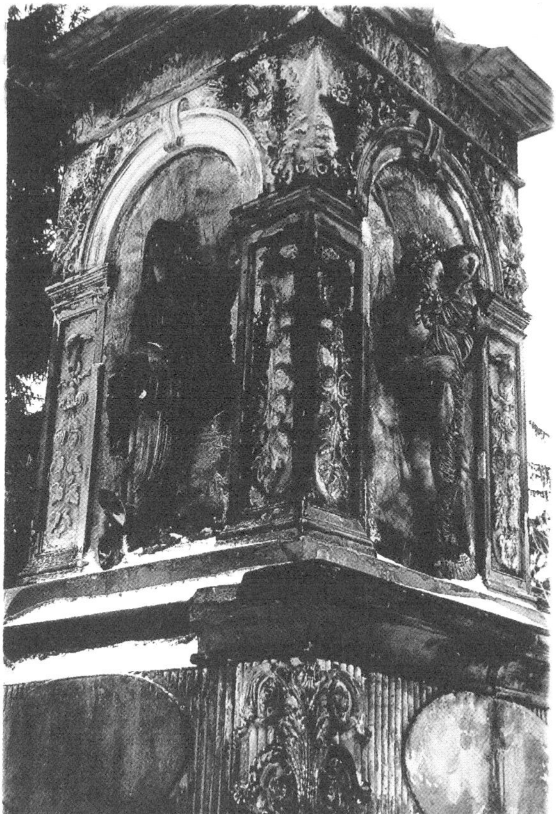

"I don't want to hurry it, but I'm so interested in getting to heaven."
—Fred Rogers (Mr. Rogers' Neighborhood)

"When this earthly tent we live in is taken down—when we die and leave these bodies—we will have a home in heaven, an eternal body made for us by God himself."
—2 Corinthians 5:1, NLT

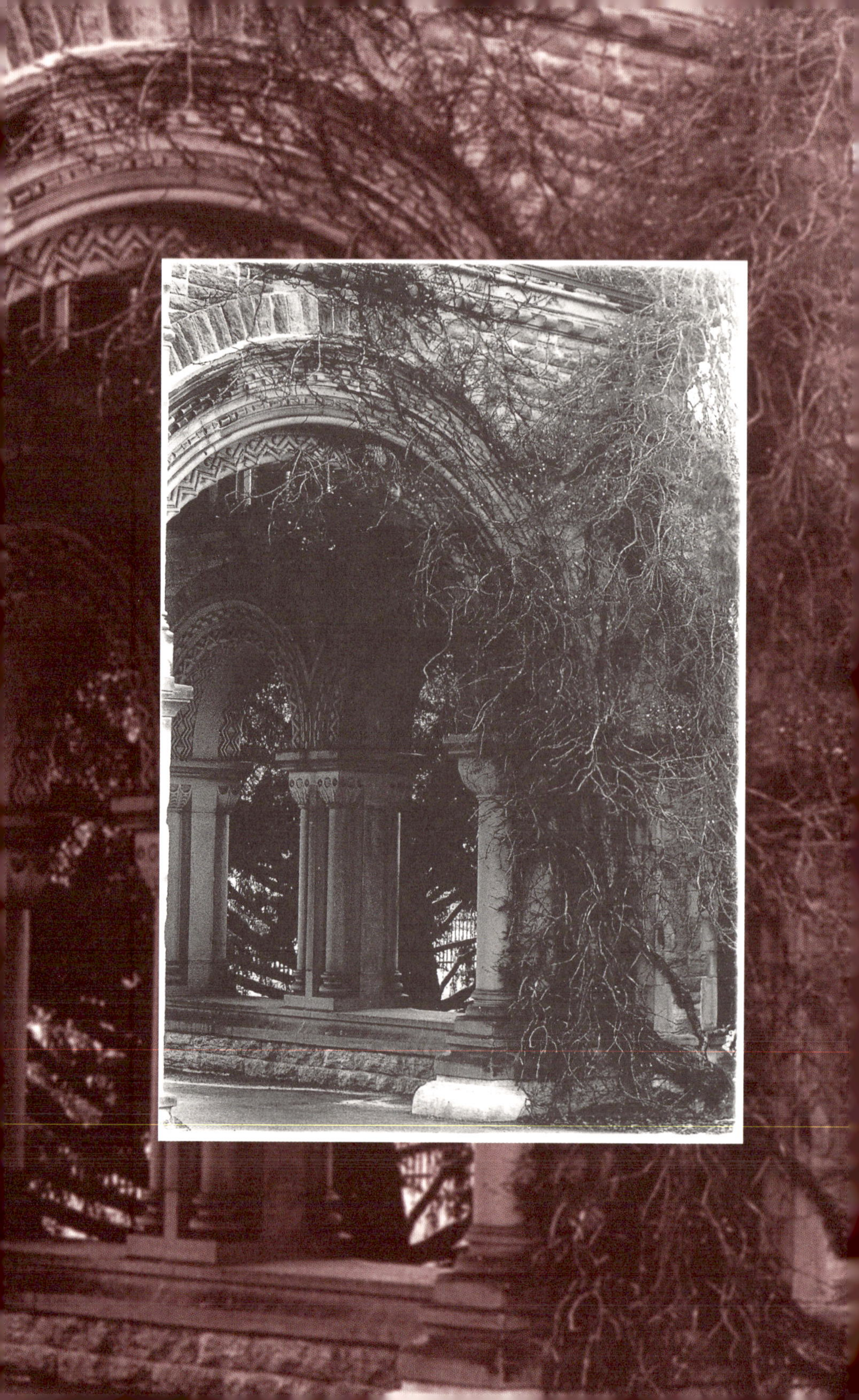

> "I AM THE GATE;
> WHOEVER ENTERS THROUGH ME
> WILL BE SAVED."
>
> —JESUS, JOHN 10:9, NIV

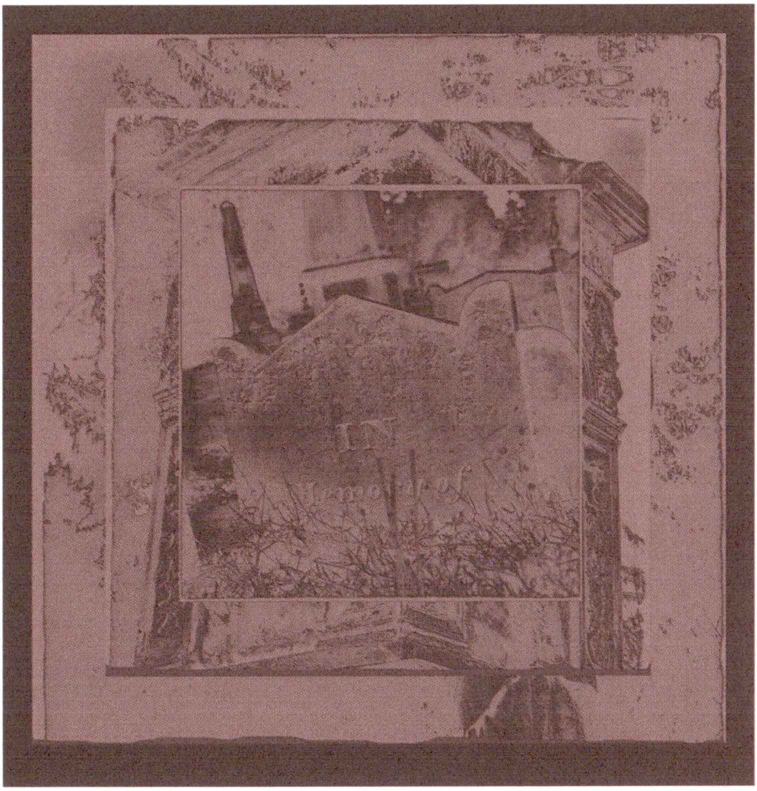

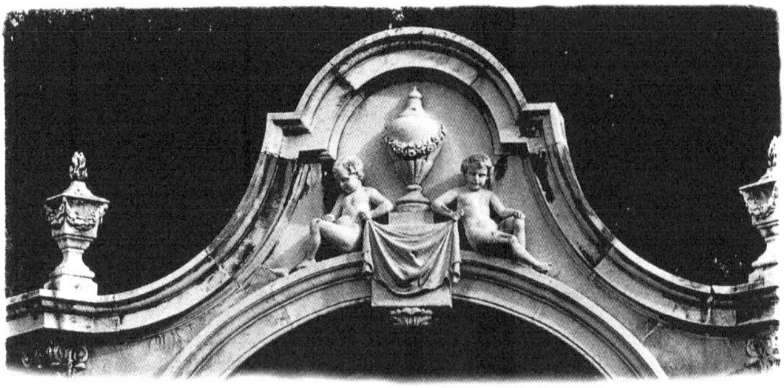

> "If by my life or death I can protect you, I will."
> —Aragorn, *The Lord of the Rings: The Fellowship of the Rings*

> "I am the resurrection and the life. He who believes in me will live, even though he dies; and whoever lives and believes in me will never die."
> —Jesus, John 11:25, 26, NIV

EPITAPH

Here lies the body
of Ann Mann;
Who lived an old woman,
And died an old Mann.
—Bath Abbey

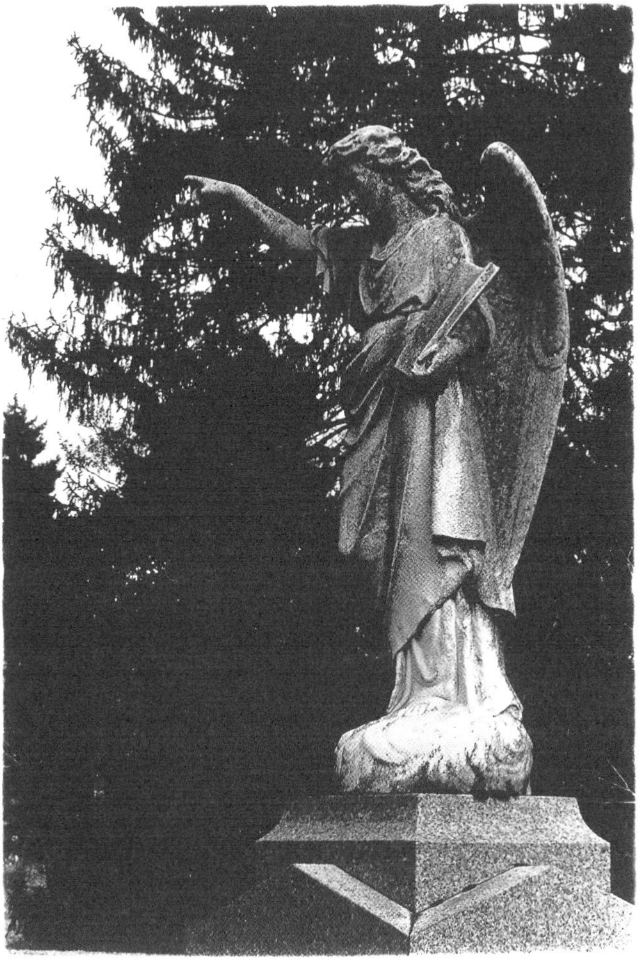

> "If I could drop dead right now, I'd be the happiest man alive."
> —Samuel Goldwyn

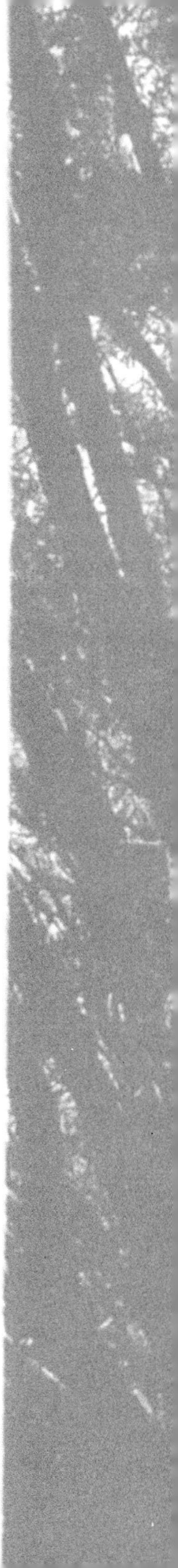

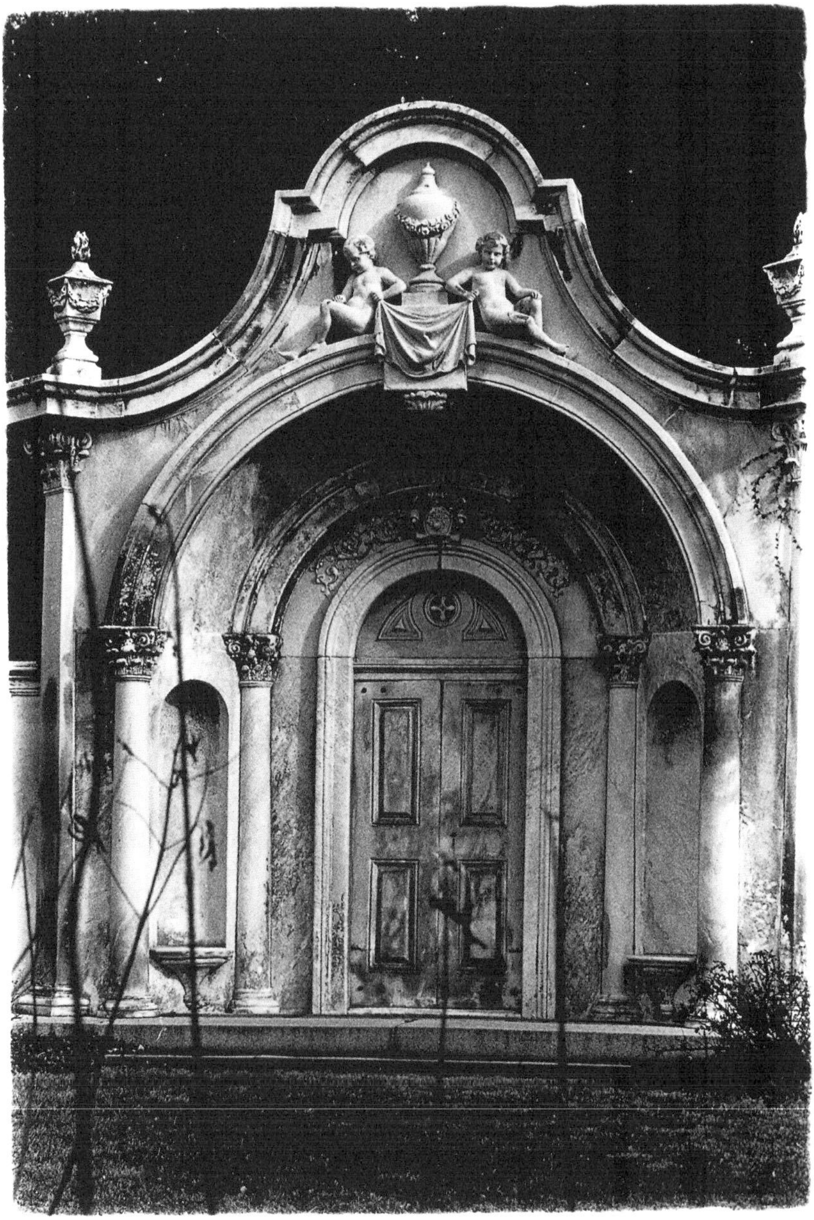

"Just play the hand you're dealt."
—Christopher Reeve

"Even when I walk through the dark valley of death, I will not be afraid, for you are close beside me."

—David to God, Psalm 23:4, NLT

PAYABLE ON DEATH

"All come from dust, and to dust all return."
—Ecclesiastes 3:20, niv

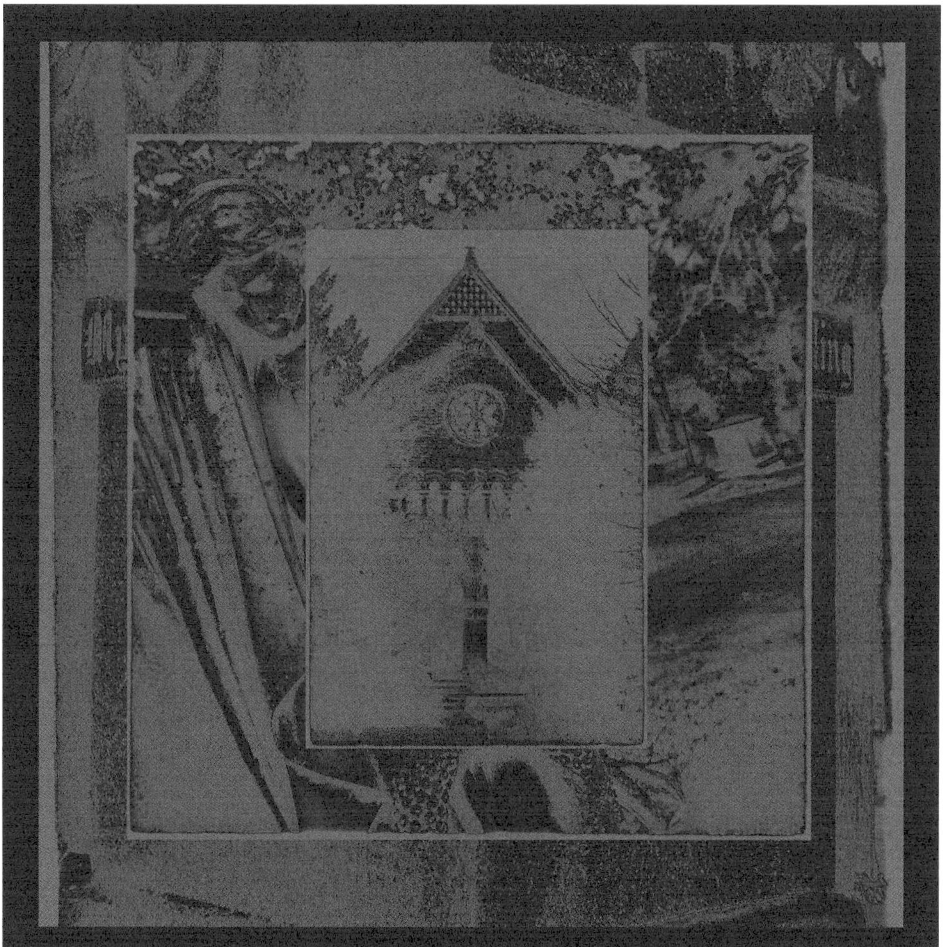

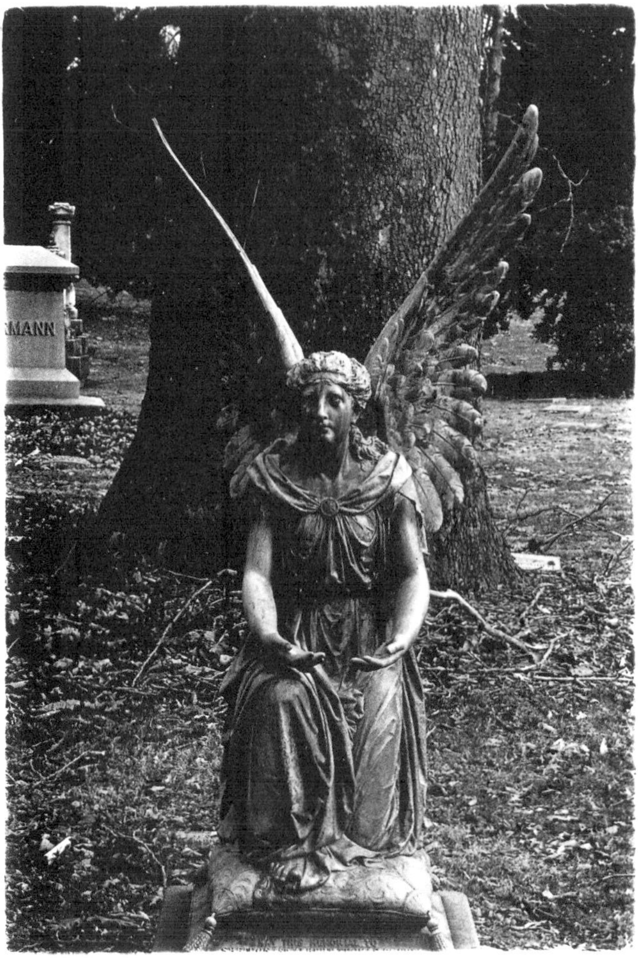

"All who are victorious will be clothed in white. I will never erase their names from the Book of Life, but I will announce before my Father and his angels that they are mine."

—Jesus, Revelation 3:5, NLT

EPITAPH

Danny Dimm was not
too bright.
He ate a stick of dynamite.
Rest in pieces.
—quoted by Joan Horton

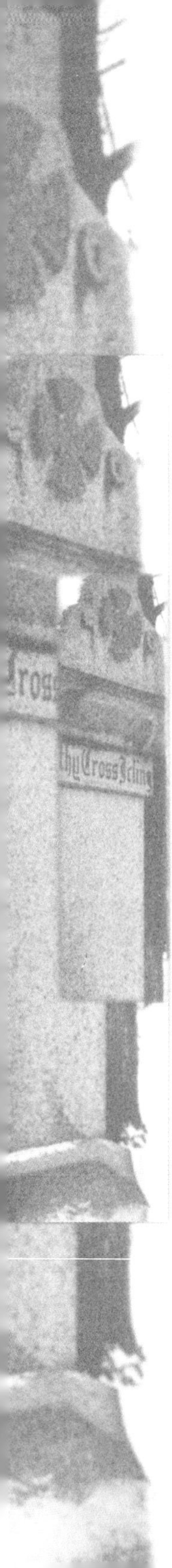
thy Cross

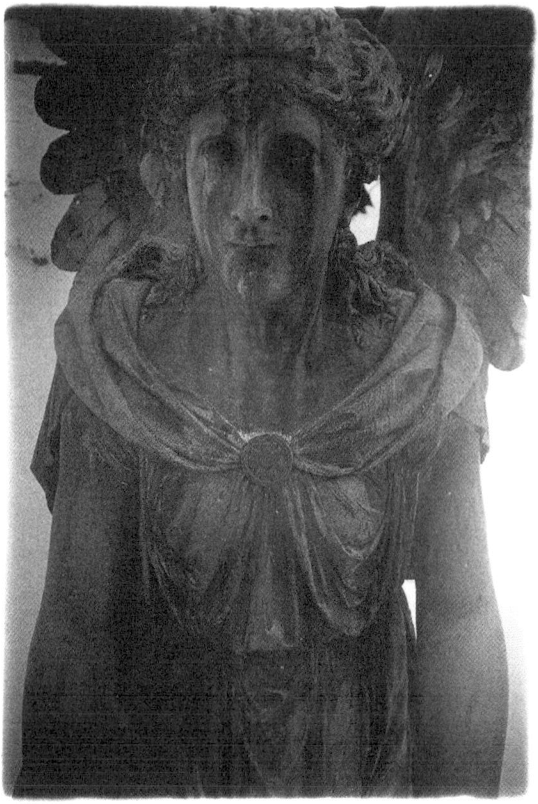

> "DO YOU KNOW WHERE THE GATES
> OF DEATH ARE LOCATED? HAVE YOU
> SEEN THE GATES OF UTTER GLOOM?"
>
> —God to Job, Job 38:17, NLT

"Most of the people here . . . don't have problems with believing in life after death. To believe in life before death— a life which is worth living—this is the difficulty."
—Mitri Raheb, minister in Bethlehem

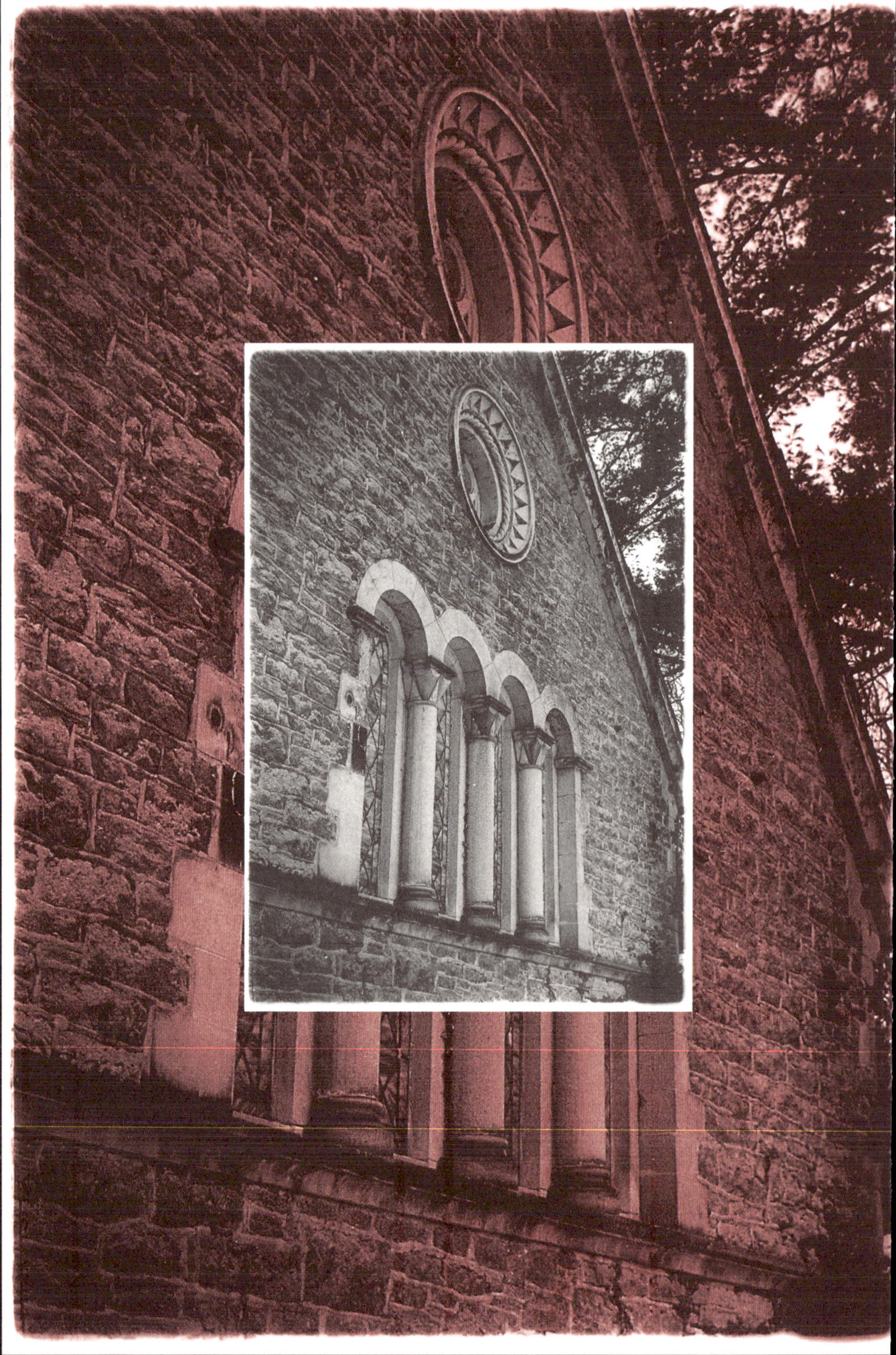

> "Satan hates you and has a terrible plan for your life."
> —Timothy Warner

> "May the LORD value my life and deliver me from all trouble."
> —David, 1 Samuel 26:24, NIV

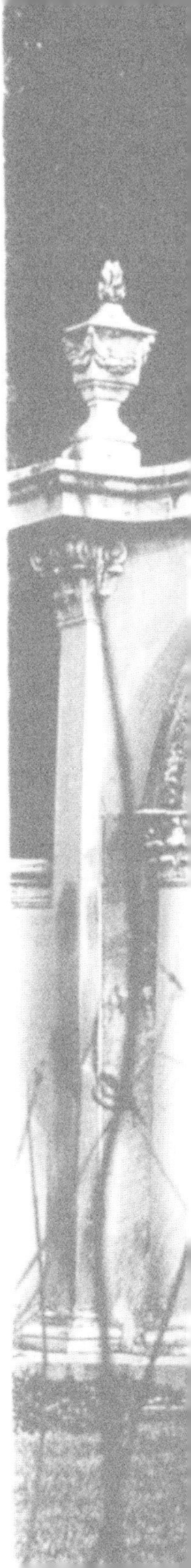

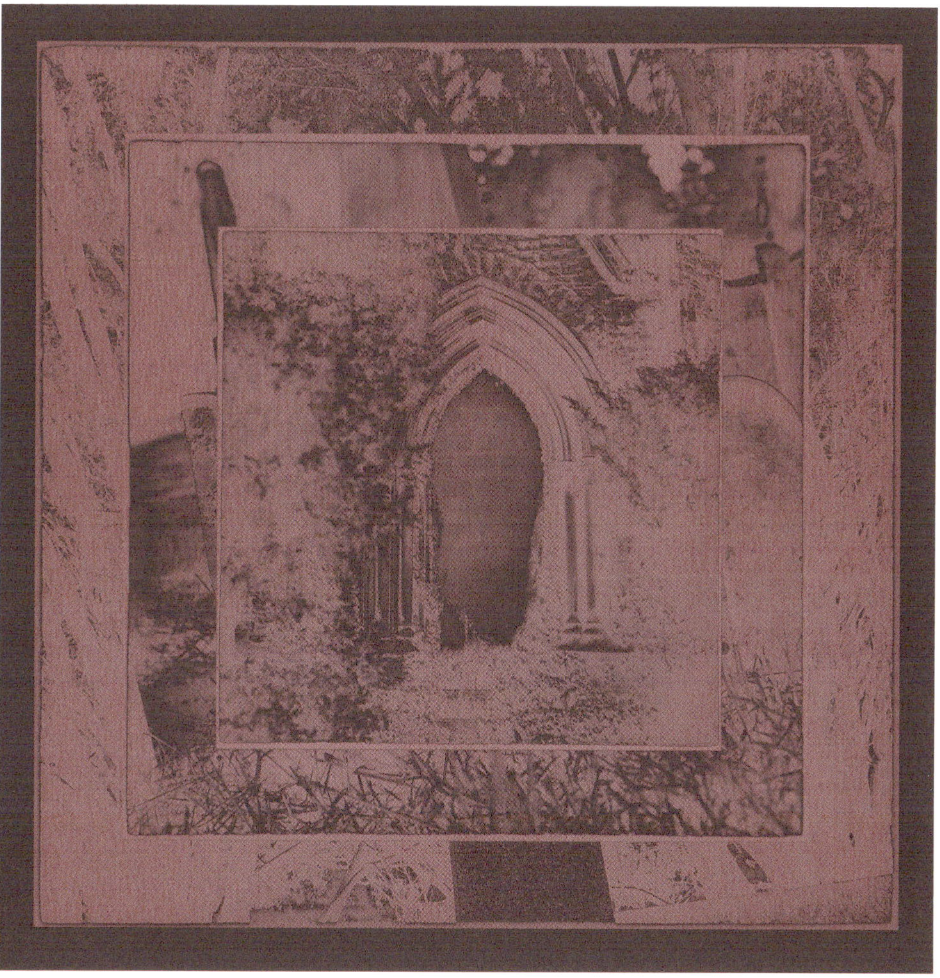

"Man's main concern is not to gain pleasure or to avoid pain, but rather to see a meaning in his life."
—Viktor Frankl

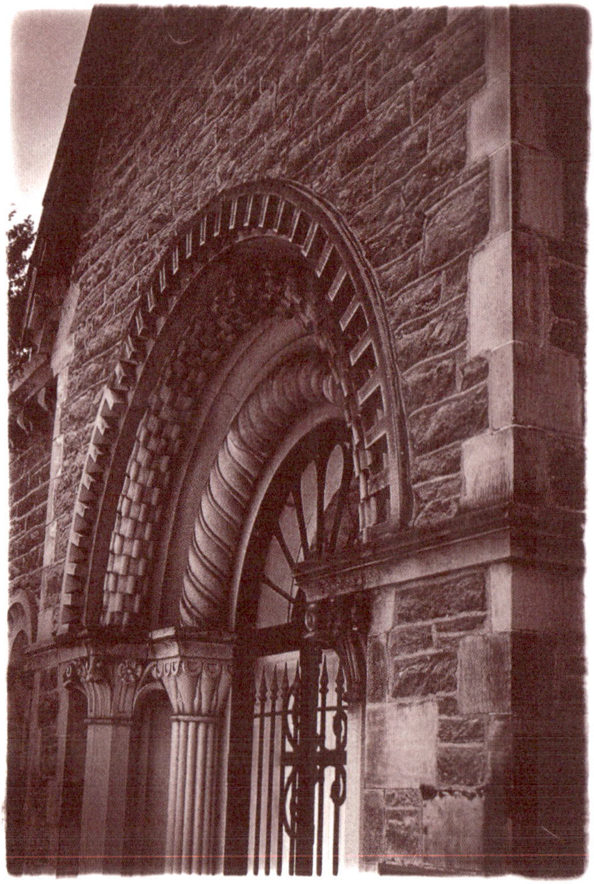

Back from the dead

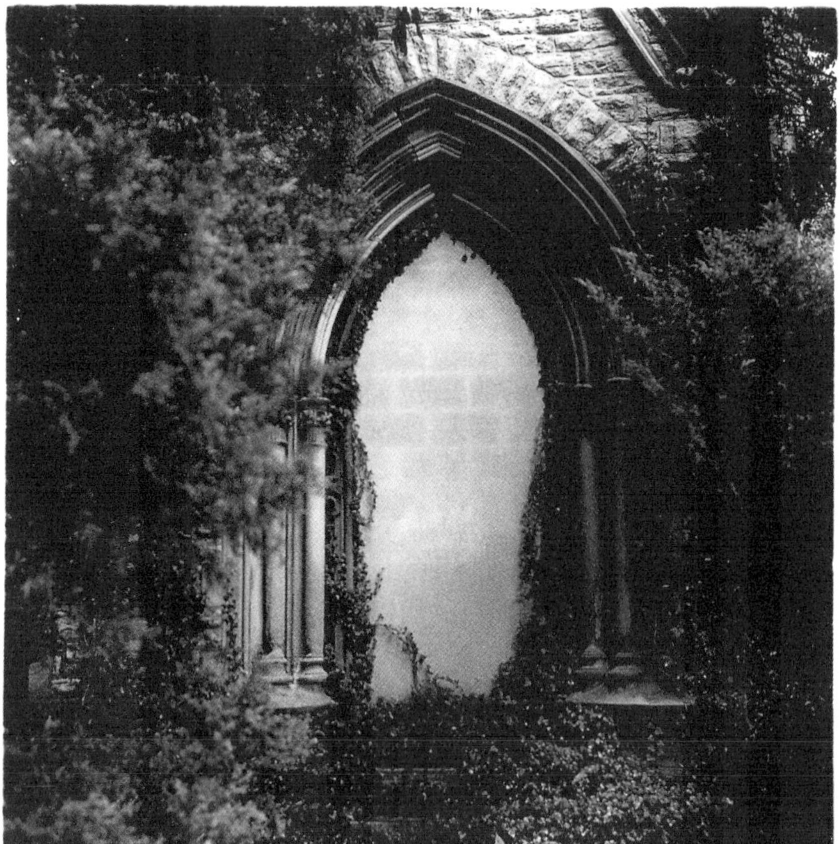

"A dead end is just a good place to turn around."
—Naomi Judd

"Neither death nor life, neither angels nor demons, neither the present nor the future, nor any powers, neither height nor depth, nor anything else in all creation, will be able to separate us from the love of God that is in Christ Jesus our Lord."
—Paul, Romans 8:38, 39, niv

"BECAUSE GOD'S CHILDREN ARE HUMAN BEINGS—MADE OF FLESH AND BLOOD—JESUS ALSO BECAME FLESH AND BLOOD BY BEING BORN IN HUMAN FORM. FOR ONLY AS A HUMAN BEING COULD HE DIE, AND ONLY BY DYING COULD HE BREAK THE POWER OF THE DEVIL, WHO HAD THE POWER OF DEATH. ONLY IN THIS WAY COULD HE DELIVER THOSE WHO HAVE LIVED ALL THEIR LIVES AS SLAVES TO THE FEAR OF DYING."
—HEBREWS 2:14, 15, NLT

BEYOND features the photography of David Strasser. A native of Cincinnati, Ohio, and graduate of Cincinnati Christian University, David is a musician, artist and freelance photographer. He owns his own business, Entertaining Angels. David lives with his wife and four children in Cincinnati.